Changing Faces
II

Darrel Dabbs

ISBN 978-1-7320846-3-6

Liberation's Publishing LLC
West Point, Mississippi
www.liberationspublishing.com

DEDICATION

First and foremost, I give all thanks to Almighty God, and I dedicate this to him because if he had not been here carrying me through these tough times and seeing me through, I wouldn't' be able to do anything of value.

I would like to dedicate this page to Shirley Buchanan, a dear and true friend who sacrificed her time and energy to develop the manuscript for this book. She supported me on this journey.

Lastly, I dedicate this to all my friends, family, and all others who seek to understand the pain involved in this type of experience.

Bless the name of the Lord!

Contents

Darrel Joe is what his friends and acquaintances called him. Something about that name that automatically set the tone of the conversation, energetic and exciting. Whenever the name Darrel Joe was mentioned, you would always think party, music concerts, or some other event that entailed food, fun, and friends!

Behind his energetic bounce and the smell of uniquely alluring cologne hid the fear and lack of confidence of a young man tormented with the reality of living with the skin changing effects of vitiligo, a condition he concealed with makeup and creating an atmosphere of good times.

During the makeup-wearing period, Darrel never exposed himself as being vulnerable or sensitive. He splurged on clothes, cars, and parties. Always a dapper dude in a suit, Darrel often wore gloves as part of his wardrobe. We always thought he liked the fashion statement he (and Michael Jackson) made. Nevertheless, being in Darrel Joe's circle of friends was a place coveted by many makeup and all.

Now that I think about it, the fact that he applied

some type of skin regimen never mattered to the friendship. However, it was clear that the bouncy, free spirited young man often referred to as Big Money Doc) was insecure with the secret of knowing his skin was changing, causing strange looking blotches to appear across his body, and in his mind, there was nothing he could do about it.

I could never imagine what the effect of having to endure this might have had on him or the effect it would have on anyone facing this physical uncertainty. Nevertheless, with the help and encouragement of his mother, Darrel Joe was unwavering in his determination and resolved to live independent of his circumstances, and he refused to give his skin ailment complete power over him.

It wasn't until he had undergone complete skin change that he developed the desire to put his story in book form as a means of helping and encouraging others who are afflicted by the traumas of vitiligo.

While he had overcome vitiligo, Darrel had not healed from the verbal abuse he suffered from various people he encountered who knew of his vulnerability in dealing with the devastation of skin and complexion change. He never quite dealt with the pain associated with the cruelty and lack of compassion coming from some of his peers. Perhaps his book is part of the healing process and his way of saying, "How do you like me now?"

He had overcome! Because he had overcome, he knew without any doubt that others could overcome it as well.

-A Friend

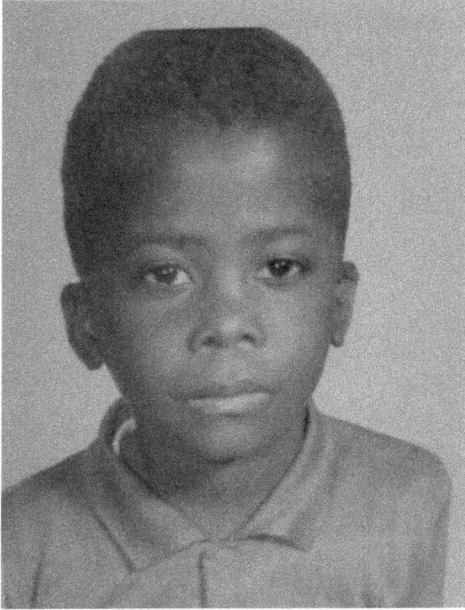

In The Beginning

I was born a twin, but my brother died at birth. I
lived, but was severely anemic and had to be given a blood
transfusion. I was sent home later with my mother, Debra
Dabbs; my father, C. D. Dabbs; and an older brother, Carl
Dabbs. I remember very little of my father being around
home with us. It was if I only had one parent. I
remember staying with my aunt Alberta Cox in Nettleton,
Mississippi, because my mother and father began having
problems.

My mother was a sharecropper and a single mother.

She worked very hard to take care of me and my older brother. She later moved to Shannon, Mississippi, met a man named U. S. McGlown, and married him. She felt she needed a husband to help raise two boys in the South. My mother and her new husband, U. S. McGlown, soon brought me and my brother to live with them in Shannon, Mississippi.

I have always worked. My stepfather gave me plenty of chores to do around the house even as a little boy. Around age thirteen, I was mowing lawns and working part-time for Robert Smith at Smith's Dairy Bar, their family business in Shannon, Mississippi. Cleaning bathrooms and picking up paper were considered honest work in those days. Today you might get cussed out if you ask someone to clean toilets and pick up paper to make extra money! It seems nowadays instead of doing honest work to make money, people would rather try and figure out how they can get their hands on yours.

I was around fifteen when I looked in the mirror and noticed a white spot around my right eye. It wasn't very noticeable, so I didn't think much of it being there. The spot appeared to get a little bigger after about a year. I saw an almost identical spot on my left eye. By this time, my lips had little white spots on them too.

At first, no one at school noticed the first spot around my right eye. My mom didn't notice, nor did I pay any attention to it. The spots spread to my left eye, my nose, and my lips, then it became a problem. My mom talked with one of her relatives about it. She told my mother that her son had the same condition, but she didn't know what it was called. She told my mother about using makeup to cover the spot. At that time, I had no idea what makeup was or how to use it. The spots were very embarrassing , so I was willing try anything. Some people were afraid of me because of my skin discoloration. They thought it was something contagious.

To help boost myself-esteem and keep others from being afraid of me, I began wearing makeup to remove the shock factor of the effects of vitiligo on one's appearance. I began wearing makeup in 1975 and wore it for twenty-two years until 1997. It took exactly twenty-three years for all the spots to disappear and my skin was one color.

Back to school, it was kind of different when I was in school. We had bullies, but kids weren't excessively mean.

There were a few who managed to poke fun and get away with it but not many. It was embarrassing enough to have spots developing on my face, and even more hurtful to be laughed at.

I remember wearing glasses at the time the spots began developing around my eyes. I told my mother that I would never take another school picture, because the spots were visible through my glasses. I guess she spoke to relatives about it, because I had a cousin that suggested using an eyebrow pencil.

Another makeup lesson. We would apply this cream, and then we would cover the spots around my eyes, lips, and nose using the eyebrow pencil. I was overwhelmed with joy. I thought, for sure this will work, and I will soon be back to normal. My mother was so proud. She too had begun to raise her expectation. She shared her feelings with a cousin, saying, "Look my son's color is coming back. I'm so happy!" I am sure my classmates were perplexed. In their mind, one day I was spotted, and the next day I looked pretty normal

As time passed the dark spots started lightening back up. I knew then that it was only temporary nothing was really working. I remember playing in what I thought was grass; but was later discovered it be poison ivy. This aggravated my vitiligo horribly. More spots appeared. Me and my makeup was there to stay going forward. I wore it every day and it became a very expensive and tedious.

Trying to save face

I bought lots and lots of cotton balls. Store clerks probably wondered who I was buying them for. If they only knew. The walls inside the half-bath where I made my face (applied makeup) were covered with brown fingerprints. It was where I had forgotten to clean my fingers before inadvertently touching the walls and other things in the room. There were so many they appeared to resemble a design on the wallpaper.

I used my index finger to apply makeup. I developed an anxiety behind my index finger and my entire situation. What if my finger became sprained or broken? How would I apply the makeup? Asking someone else to do it was certainly out of the question. I was never caught outside without my makeup. I was not taking any chances, I had to keep the bullying down to a minimum. So I started my day a lot earlier than others. If I had an appointment at nine, I had to start getting ready at six. Patience became a virtue in an entirely different way.

I continued working at Smith's Dairy Bar and made money to buy my own makeup. I am proud of my stepfather for teaching me the value of work at an early age. Besides my mother didn't pamper me because of my condition. She encouraged me to work despite it.

When I was in the tenth grade, I began working for LIFT Inc. during the summer. This provided the extra money need to help with household expenses. At this time, I didn't have a girlfriend and I shied away from people as much as possible. Work became my mistress. I would wake up to makeup, you might say.

The night job came along during my senior year. I worked from two thirty in the afternoon until eleven at night. That wasn't enough. SO I got a job delivering newspaper, which made it impossible for me to have free time, and that was how I wanted it. I didn't want to have any time to think about my skin. I just needed enough time to get made up, to "hide" it. I didn't want to focus on the way it was changing and affecting my life.

It was like a nightmare. One day everything was

normal, and the next day it was total chaos! I went from being normal to a man who applied makeup every morning. I started wearing long-sleeve shirts no matter how hot it was. I had to keep a close eye on the makeup to make sure it didn't run. It wasn't easy. I am stronger because of it.

Darrel Dabbs

Growing Up

I bought my first car, a black and white 1965 Chevrolet, in my senior year in high school. I was working two jobs as a means of escaping a problem that wasn't going away. I was black and white.

Despite the new car, I began to think that perhaps it would never get the girl I could call my sweetheart. I could not enjoy the fun of a swimming pool like my peers. I avoided eating out, and I didn't dare consider having sleepovers with friends for fear of waking up to makeup stains on the pillow. I was paranoid!

On top of my personal issue, I received a kick in the stomach that hurt more than anything. I was being told that I couldn't graduate with my class because I lacked a credit and a half to complete my high school requirements. What? Was there a reason why no one told me that earlier in the year? Did they not want to give me the opportunity to get it? When I arrived to rehearse with my class, I was told I couldn't march. I had already purchased my class ring. At least they couldn't take that away.

I made my life work without the diploma; nevertheless, I kept two jobs and attended summer school. I failed summer school, no diploma. I didn't it around and feel sorry for myself. I just kept working.

Only a few people at my job knew I had vitiligo. My makeup was in place, and I was in total disguise. No illness, no doctors, but my skin kept changing everywhere! I started out using twenty ounces of makeup a day; now it was up to forty ounces.

On October 10, 1978, I begin working for Sunshine Mills in Tupelo, Mississippi, where my hourly pay changed from $1.54 an hour to $2.70. I worked in the grain elevator. It was nasty work but turned out to have good pay after a while. I was very dedicated and no longer needed the second job. I was getting long hours at Sunshine Mills. This job gave me a new look on life even though I was somewhat limited. I thank God that he gave me the strength and the courage to work despite my condition. I would rise every morning like clockwork put on my makeup, and off to work I would go.

I worked consistently for ten years at Sunshine Mills, not missing a day. Work became such therapy for me that I would rather be there than any place else. I was still living at home with my mother, helping her with bills. The rest of my money I used to party on the weekends, help others in need, pay tithes at church, and spend on other things I enjoyed.

It's true money can't buy happiness. Despite the money I was making, it didn't change the fact that I had a serious problem. I was hooked on wearing makeup and lots of it.

In 1982, I married my wife, Sharon Betts, who had a son prior to our marriage. I moved out of my mother's house and got a rental house for my new family. I decided to take the makeup off and show her what I looked like. It had a devastating effect on the marriage. I had not been true to her because I had not been true to myself regarding what was happening to me . I concealed an important part of myself from her. This was wrong.

Neither of us was ready for marriage. I don't think love had anything to do with it. Neither of us married for the right reason. I was vulnerable, and so fearful that I would never have a normal relationship that I hid myself from the one I would spend the rest of my life with.

I think she wanted to get away from home. She knew I had a good job. I was nice. I knew how to treat women. I wasn't dating anyone else, because I was shy and I believed that my skin would be a downfall to romance. We stayed together for about a year. It ended with lots of arguments. Though my wife knew of my condition, she didn't seem to care until she was angry.

When my wife would get angry, she would call me all sorts of "sporty" names, including "salt and pepper," which is much nicer than the other names she would call me. I don't know if her son ever questioned her about why she was calling me those names or whether he ignored the names. Maybe it was because I was so skillful at hiding my true color from him. I really didn't know what he would think of me.

I knew there had to be more to marriage than what we had, so we separated, and I filed for divorce. After a little while, she came back, but we could never make it work. I moved back home with my mother until 1983. In 1983 I purchased a brand new two-bedroom mobile home with one and a half baths. It was my dream bachelor's pad! Working hard and faithfully, I was able to pay for it. Around the same time, I had purchased a 1977 Trans Am T-top. My ex-wife and her son moved back! Go figure.

The one thing I always wanted to do was to go to Baskin-Robbins, sit down, and eat a big cone of ice cream, but I was afraid that my makeup would rub off my lips. I couldn't, and didn't, ever do that. What a wall of deception I had built around myself. Even at work I would carry a mirror to make sure my makeup would stay on. I would from time to time put makeup on my lips because of the discolorations.

I kept working very hard for long hours and did not pay attention to my health. I ignored the signs in my body. It was work, work, work. One week I did one hundred hours. Then I started eating less and less; my immune system was shutting down. My appetite left; I couldn't eat anything. Nothing I ate would stay down. I was very sick.

Escaping Death

I had divorced my wife. In my zeal to prove life must go on, I asked a friend to introduce me to a young lady. She came to my house, and we talked. She seemed like a nice lady, so I allowed her to move in with me. To be honest, I don't think she even liked me. She was very cunning, and I had everything of material value she wanted.

She could see I had a good job and a nice house. She also knew I was self-conscious of my skin discoloration. My sensitivity was what she skillfully used to build her web of lies and deceit. Out of respect for her I won't use her real name. We'll call her Pattie.

She did all the things she sensed I needed. For instance, I've always had trouble with women because of my insecurity. I had divorced the only woman I had been physically close to. So I was vulnerable and would react favorably to all good deeds done toward me. Pattie would cook for me and clean. When I came home from work, she would meet me at the door wearing lingerie and a huge smile. I should have known it was all too good to be true.

I found myself getting sick and even having to go to the doctor, and they couldn't find anything wrong me. Once I was off from work for two days. It still had not sunk in. Little things just kept happening, and I didn't have the presence of mind to figure it out. One night we go into a huge argument. My money and credit cards were stolen. As it turned out, she had maxed out my credit cards. That was the last straw. I asked her to leave, but she didn't leave right away.

She had alienated all my true friends. They hardly came around anymore. I may not have sunk into the shape I was in if my friends had been regular visitors. Pattie had a sinister plan. One day I came home to a supper she had fixed. She had set aside a specific plate for me. Needless to say, after being robbed blind, I was very conscious of what was going on around me. She thought I ate the food, but I didn't. I was already suspicious that she was trying to take me out. It was strange that she still wouldn't leave. If I had been caught stealing money and credit cards I couldn't stay around.

She had hamburgers prepared for me another day. I didn't dare eat them. It was pretty obvious that the hamburgers were for me while she ordered food from Smith's Dairy Bar for herself. Yes, it was quite clear that the hamburgers were to be my last supper. I made up my mind that I was not going to eat those hamburgers, and I'm glad I didn't.

A couple of friends came over to help me move her out of my house. One of my friends asked me if I had something to eat. I told him that she had cooked some hamburgers, but I told him that I would not eat them. I believed something was wrong with them. He bagged hamburgers and took them home to eat later because I didn't have any bread. It was divinely ordered that when he got home, his mother had cooked supper, and he didn't have to eat the hamburgers. He put the meat from the hamburger in his refrigerator.

He had a dog named Queen, he gave her and her puppy the hamburgers the next morning. He didn't know that the hamburgers had been laced with poison. They had been intended for me.

Sadly, Queen and puppy died. My friend called me and told me that it was good that we didn't eat those hamburgers. He told me what had happened to his dogs. That was another proof that God will take care of me. Through this I learned that you should never become so insecure that you let people take advantage of you.

I tried to be normal and I allowed people to take advantage of me. This time it would have cost me my life if God had not taken care of me. I have always made a special effort to be nice to people strangers or not. Perhaps I tried too hard. There are always people waiting to take advantage of you.

Ignoring The Signs

I started feeling really bad after work early one Saturday morning. I felt so tired that I didn't have the strength to get off the sofa. So I rested a minute,; I felt a little better, and I managed to get into bed.

All day on Sunday I felt sluggish. I still didn't know I was sick. I just waved it off as being tired, so I just rested. Monday came. I put my makeup on, and I was right back at work. I didn't feel well, but I was determined to work. I rested a little and worked a little. Accustomed to working life I made up my mind that I would try to make it another week, so I did. When I got off work that Saturday morning, I drove myself straight to the North Mississippi Medical Center (NMMC). They immediately admitted me.

I was diagnosed with anemia, and the next day I was given two pints of blood and lots of test. My makeup

21

stayed on overnight because I wasn't able to wash it off. Even if I had the strength to remove it, I wouldn't have washed it off. I was in a hospital, and the last thing I wanted was for those doctors and nurses to see the effect vitiligo was having on my body.

I called my brother and told him where I was and asked him to pass by my house and bring my makeup to the hospital. The hospital staff noticed I had makeup on my face and told me I had to remove it before going to surgery. I removed it, but as soon as I was able I rushed to the makeup jar.

I was in the hospital for about a week. Each morning I made sure I put my makeup on. After being off from work for a short time and taking medication, I started feeling normal and went back to work. About a month later I felt myself getting sick again. This time it was really serious.

You can do harm to your body while trying to do good. You can work too hard. You can live in denial. You can get no rest, and most of all, you can ignore the signs. All these things can be devastating to your health and even take your life.

I think I just got carried away with making lots of money, having my own house, a nice car, nice clothes, that I didn't think about my annual checkups with the doctor. I felt myself getting sick at work. I had begun coughing a lot. I started taking antibiotics, but that made it worse, so one day I clocked out early from work. On my way home, I stopped and got pizza from William's grocery. I tried to eat it, but I just couldn't. It made me sick to even smell it.

I made it home and lay down. The next morning, it tried to get up and put my makeup on. No matter how sick I was, I always reached for the makeup jar first. I was determined not to be seen without it. At that time, my skin color had changed everywhere; I was almost totally white.

My supervisor called to see whether I was able to come to work. I just could not go back to work. I was doing bad. I was experiencing some type of fluid buildup. My feet had become swollen. I didn't know what was wrong,. I just lay around all day hoping that I would get better.

All night long I kept spitting up fluid. At last, I was

able to sleep sitting upright in a recliner. This kept the fluid form clogging my lungs, and it continued for two days, it wasn't getting any better so I called a friend and asked her to take me to the hospital. I told her I was really sick. I was so weak I could hardly lift my hands to put my makeup on, but I managed. I hadn't eaten anything in three days which, in retrospect, might explain the weakness.

When I arrived at the hospital, they admitted me immediately. I told the nurse I had not eaten in three days and was very hungry. She was nice enough to share a sandwich she had brought to work for her lunch. I tried to eat it, and that's when all hell broke loose! Doctors around me were tearing my clothes off, and that was the last thing I remember.

I was told my heart had stopped beating, and they called code blue. I woke up in the intensive care unit with a ventilator connected through the night to keep me breathing. The next morning, the nurses told me my breathing was better. I remained in intensive care for eight days, and still remained in the hospital from February 13 to April 1.

Doctors still didn't know what was wrong with me or how to treat my condition. They must have decided on giving me some type of chemo or radiation because my hair started shedding really badly. Only God knows all the things I was being treated for. It appears they were experimenting, treating me for everything except my real condition trying to find the cause of my ailment.

One day, the doctor came into the room and asked if they could give me a skin test, and thank God they did! That's when they found out I had tuberculosis (TB). They actually thought I had cancer. I guess from all indications, it did look like cancer. I had told my doctor that my father had cancer, and I guess that was the main reason she treated me for cancer.

Nevertheless, it is imperative for doctors to be sure before administering certain medications or before ordering particular treatments. I could have died from all the wrong medications I received. God kept me alive, and I am truly grateful to him. I was finally dismissed from the hospital. I entered the hospital weighting 170 to 175 pounds. When I was released, I barely weighed 100 pounds. I had no strength to walk. My ex-wife invited me to live with her until I regained some of my strength and could to live on my own, so I did. She was nice enough to help me to and from the bathroom and to cook and care for me while I recovered.

Healing and Reviving

I had to have help at home from April 1 to September, for five months. It was a strange and awesome experience to have to learn to walk all over again. My color started to change fast while I was in the hospital. I couldn't use makeup; neither did I have the strength to get out of bed. Makeup was the last thing on my mind. I wasn't sure what was causing my drastic color change. It could have been the medication. I'm really not sure. All I know is when I got home and was able to look in the mirror, I was shocked.

My neck and everything were white. How could I buy enough makeup to cover all that? I couldn't not any longer. I knew for a fact that I couldn't use any more makeup. It would take too long, cost too much. I just had to accept the fact that I couldn't hide my skin color anymore. I could if I stayed at home forever and talked to people through my doors and never showed my face. Everyone who knows me would tell you that's impossible!

I never gave up. I made up my mind to go back to work; I just didn't know when. In fact, I was even more determined to go back to work. Up until then I didn't want to be seen without makeup, but it felt good to be free of the struggles of keeping a false face. I was somewhat relieved to know I didn't have to do it anymore.

For five months I was home watching TV, taking medications, and constantly bracing myself on the walls and furniture trying to walk. I could no longer drive my car, but I was determined to regain my strength. I knew deep down inside of me that with my determination and GOD's help things would change for me.

One of my medications was prednisone, and this gave me a big appetite and put some meat back on my bones. I rested a lot and started getting stronger and stronger. I still felt tired most of the time, though. Then I got the news that I needed to come back to work or I would be fired.

In September, I was back to work. I got joked a lot about my color. My coworkers told me that I was turning white. I worked from seven in the morning until noon until I got better and got all my strength back. I worked for six months without missing a day.

I had already checked on disability and found I was eligible for it. I really thought hard about it. Finally, I made a decision to quit the job after twenty one years. I didn't t want to risk getting fired. I've never regretted the decision I made to leave the workforce. I knew my health was not the same and never would be again.

I was home again, feeling much better, thinking of what I could do to stay busy and not feel lazy. Travel is one thing that came to mind. I have nice car (BMW): that might be a good reason to take a road trip. I also became more active in church.

I could wear white shirts and didn't have to worry about getting makeup on my collar. I didn't know how much bondage I was in. I was bound to wearing makeup like and addiction. I never felt so relieved in my entire life. Finally I didn't have to portray myself as someone I'm wasn't. For the first time in a long time I could be myself.

You should be yourself no matter what condition

you're in whether you feel good about yourself or not. If you neglect being yourself, it will become painful for you later in life. Be yourself and find a way to be happy with yourself.

For the first time in my life, I began going out to eat. This was something I wouldn't do before because of the makeup. I fished a little and mowed lawns. I just felt free. I guess I was doing too much too soon because I started feeling tired again, but I didn't want to go back to the doctor.

My condition didn't get any better. I went back to doctor to find that my blood count had dropped too low. I had to have two pints of blood again, and I was put back on prednisone. This was when I had to accept that I wasn't the same anymore. I know it was really up to me to take care of myself. I went back to the doctor for a regular checkup and she decided that I needed surgery to remove my spleen; she said that this would or should stop my blood count from falling.

Getting My Tattoo

Even though I didn't graduate with my class, I was invited to our twentieth-year class reunion. I painted my lips real good; my face was made up. I was looking good all made up outside but a wreck inside. I never ate out because I knew it would be a problem, mostly of me worrying about wearing makeup off. I ate mostly finger foods at the reunion so that I could eat with my fingers and guide the food into my mouth without touching my lips. This way lipstick would stay on.

Just as I always feared, it didn't matter how careful I was; it was still impossible for the coloring to stay on lips (the photo will verify this). After the reunion, I read an advertisement in the newspaper that said I could get permanent color for my lips through tattoo art. My color was leaving, and I was desperate to stop wearing makeup. I wanted to enjoy the simple things. I decided to have my lips tattooed.

I went to the tattoo artist's house. She didn't have a parlor. I didn't even ask her if she was licensed. I found her through the advertisement. She had treated other vitiligo customers like me and her work looked very professionally done. She was shocked when she saw me. She thought that I getting tattoos all over my body. She said, "I've never done one with as much skin discoloration as you."

However, I didn't go there for my entire body to be tattooed, only my lips. So she started the treatments, which consisted of injecting my lips with what I assumed to be some type of a needle. I wasn't asleep, and as you can imagine that it was very, very painful. I really didn't care how painful it was because now I was thinking how I could take the girls out to eat without being embarrassed. Now my lips would hold their color if it was successful. Wow! Was I happy!

When I took the first treatment, my lips were swollen and sore for several days. It was very painful. I think I paid $300 for the first treatment and $300 for the final treatment. I go sick and couldn't go back, but the tattoo I had really helped my lips. She did enough for them to blend with my color and not stand out with the pinkish look. I was satisfied with what she did. Now my face has totally change; the color of my lips still blends with the color of my face.

The Tanning Bed

The doctor had prescribed a medication that he thought would bring the pigmentation back into my skin, and he instructed me to lie in the sun for an hour thirty minutes on my face and thirty minutes on my back. I remember seeing a little color change on my arms and legs, but it didn't last. There wasn't a major improvement. My face never changed. I needed my face and hands to change, but it never happened.

In 1988 when I got my Christmas bonus, I came to the conclusion that lying out in the sun was very embarrassing. I thought, Since I have some extra money from the Christmas bonus, I'll tan inside my house. So I purchased a suntan bed for $900.

At first, it seemed I had solved my problem. My hands and legs had begun to show great improvement, some good signs. Dark spots were forming on my skin. It was reassuring because I had the privacy of doing this for as long as it took without being seen.

One night after work I came home very tired but determined to be faithful to getting the job done. I lay inside my suntan bed facedown for fifteen minutes. I should have done fifteen minutes on my back, but being tired, I fell asleep. I had second-degree burns when I awakened.

I could barely walk. The next day, my mother and brother came over and carried me to the doctor. He prescribed some type of cream for my skin and some pain pills. I was off from work for a few days. It was over for a while no more sun tanning. I figured out it wasn't going to work anyway. It wasn't normal for a black person to have a suntan bed. A white friend came and started using it. At least it helped someone. After that, I just left it in the back room of my home. I never used it again.

In 1992, I was still searching to see if I could find something or someone to help me. Someone referred another dermatologist to me. I called him and told him my condition and ask him if he could help me. He said some reassuring things to me; I was willing to try almost anything. I set up an appointment; he started giving me treatments. I had to take some medication, take my clothes off, and get inside a box. It reminded me of my suntan bed, except lights were all around it. I didn't have to lie down, so therefore, I didn't have to turn.

From back to front, the lights were all around me. I paid $125 each time I got into the box. I remember taking more than five treatments, and it was really looking good. The color was returning rapidly, but it was a little too expensive to pay $250 a week for two treatments. My insurance company said they wouldn't cover cosmetic procedures.

I did see more color on my legs and arms, but my face remained the same. There were still no changes to my face and hands. Therefore, it was not feasible to continue treatment that did not meet my expectations. Everything worked out fine for about six months. Then all of a sudden, my blood count dropped again.

I changed doctors. He ran a battery of tests, and to his surprise, he found that my spleen had grown back. I needed two pints of blood. I was hospitalized and given medication to keep my blood count up. I had surgery to remove my spleen a second time.

The test also showed polyps on my colon that were later determined to be noncancerous. I was taken to my room, only to begin bleeding from the surgery. The odor of it was awful. They took me back into surgery. I had developed an infection that had to be cleaned out, and a portion of my colon had to removed. The doctor said I had some typed of leak, and in order to regulate my bowels, I would have to wear a colostomy bag.

I was hospitalized for about two months. I was given home health care for about a month after being released from the hospital. They would do basic medical things like change my bandages and clean the wounds, and they also educated me about the colostomy bag.

Well things again changed a little bit. I was limited because of the colostomy bag. I had to take care of it on time for about three to six months. I was hospitalized again for a low blood count. I had to have two more pints of blood.

Still on prescription drugs, I headed home afterwards to heal. The one thing I was fighting with was a low blood count. I was still in and out of the doctor's office and the hospital all the time. Life wasn't normal anymore.

Activities had slowed down tremendously. I couldn't attend church regularly. I went to a few games though I couldn't go outside as much. I didn't travel long distances at all anymore because of the attached bag. I had to always be cautious of my blood count. It would drop anytime, anywhere, so I stared close to home for fear of that happening. If and when it did, I knew I would have to be hospitalized. My life was uncertain and filled with change and adjustment for the next several years.

I was off from work by 2001, living in a single wide that I bought in 1983. It was very old, and I couldn't see it lasting another twenty. I would drive to Tupelo to shop. I passed by a mobile home store. It hit me all at once to stop and look at a particular one I saw. I stopped, and I really fell in love with it. I assumed I wouldn't qualify because I was now on fixed income. I was on disability.

When I talked to the sales person, she replied, "This is a good day for you! We have a $7,000 discount on this house today." I sat down and did the paperwork, and I got the house that same day. I know that was God.

Life had begun to give me some good things in exchange for some of the pain I had experienced. The new house was a sign that things were looking up, or it was a sign that I was just too suborn to quit.

A Few More Complications

In 2009, I still had to war the colostomy bag. I am constantly wrestling with this blood disorder. One morning I was at the laundromat drying my clothes (I only have a washer at home). A lady came into the Laundromat to wash clothes for her mother. I never meet a stranger, so I struck up a conversation with her because I love to talk. I was showing her my article in the newspaper; she thought it was very interesting.

She began to tell me she had written her father's biography. I asked her if she could help me write my book. I asked her if she would stop by my house and look at my photographs and some more information, and she said she would.

I thought now I know this was an act of God. I didn't know her; she didn't know me. But she was willing to

41

help me. I guess it's good I don't meet strangers. I didn't even know that she had written a book, but sometimes our steps are ordered by God, and this time mine was.

Things started looking up for me; my blood count was staying up longer. I was really excited about my book. I started talking to people and showing them my articles and my pictures. People were becoming exited along with me. I don't know if I got too excited or what, but all of a sudden my blood count fell, and I was back in the hospital for a few days. I was released on Wednesday, a day before Thanksgiving.

I had to have the assistance of home health care again. One day I started running a high fever; I just didn't feel good. I was admitted back into the hospital. I was back at home in time for Thanksgiving. I started feeling better.

One morning, I decided to drive to Walmart and pick up a few personal items. When I started walking in the parking lot, I saw a black bag in shopping cart; I picked it up and looked inside for some ID. When I opened it, I saw credit cards and a personal checkbook. I immediately carried the purse into Walmart's customer service area.

The lady was already at the booth inquiring about her missing purse. I spoke up and said, "Ma'am, I found your purse outside in a shopping cart!" She was very excited. I am proud I was the one who found it because not everyone is honest. I have always watched out for women; Countless time I have warned women about leaving their purses unattended.

In 2010, I was still under the doctor's care. I continued with some home health care, still having complications. Suddenly, an overgrown bump on my face grew into a rising. My doctor did outpatient surgery to remove it. I did not have to hospitalized, thank God. I met with the lady again in Okolona, Mississippi, with more pictures, and she wrote other information about me. When she came to my house, she asked me to demonstrate how I used the makeup. I thought that was strange. Being a woman, I thought she knew, but I found out that she didn't know anything about makeup because she had never worn any. I showed her how I made up my face and eyes. She was absolutely amazed.

She started writing the book. After giving her some of the information and being so excited about the book, I didn't hear anything from the lady for a long time; no phone calls, no nothing. I didn't know what to think. I felt a little down, but I never really lost the faith. All I could do was wait it out. Then I found out that the lady was sick and had been hospitalized. This brought me a little relief, knowing that she hadn't just changed her mind about writing the book.

I am still under the doctor's care, and my blood count is being closely monitored. I'm hoping that I will never have to be given blood again. To my surprise, I received a phone call from the lady writing the book for me. She said she is out of the hospital and doing pretty well, and she told me she is now ready to finish writing the book. Oh boy, was I happy! Patience plays a vital role in the outcome when you are depending on help from someone else.

I always thought that with everything I've experienced with vitiligo and other health issues, if I could just write a book my story could help a lot of vitiligo victims and hopefully prevent them from suffering some of the things I've suffered. I'm a living witness that God will hear and answer prayers.

I had an interview that ran in the Northeast

Mississippi Daily Journal concerning my condition. I carried the article with me everywhere I went because the complete face change caused me to be mistaken for a white man. I kept the article and pictures with me to prove that I didn't always look like I do now. The article was part of my proof.

I'm glad I remained patient through the trial of waiting. Now I can send a clear message to other victims of vitiligo, and maybe the message in this book will strengthen you. Hopefully, you won't have to go through some of the things I have done through. And if you do, you'll have more courage to do it.

Darrel Dabbs

What is Vitiligo

Vitiligo (pronounced vit-ill-EYE-go) is a pigmentation disorder in which melanocytes (the cells that make pigment) in the skin are destroyed. As a result, white patches appear on the skin in different parts of the body. Similar patches also appear on both the mucous membranes (tissues that line the inside of the mouth and nose) and the retina (inner layer of the eyeball). The hair that grows on areas affected by vitiligo sometimes turns white.

The cause of vitiligo is not known, but doctors and researchers have several different theories. There is strong evidence that people with vitiligo inherit a group of three genes that make them susceptible to depigmentation. In some cases, the hair color changes the color of your hair, your eyebrows, eyelashes, etc.

The most widely accepted view is that

depigmentation occurs because vitiligo is an autoimmune disease a disease in which a person's immune system reacts against the body's own organs or tissues. People's bodies produce proteins called cytokines that, in vitiligo, alter their pigment producing cells and cause these cells to die. Another theory is that melanocytes destroy themselves.

Finally, some people have reported that a single event such as sunburn or emotional distress triggered vitiligo; however, these events have not been scientifically proven as causes of vitiligo.

Who is Affected by Vitiligo?

About 0.5 to 1 percent of the world's population, or as many as 65 million people, have vitiligo. In the United States, 1 to 2 million people have the disorder. Half the people who have vitiligo develop it before age twenty; most develop it before their fortieth birthday. The disorder affects both sexed and all races equally; however, it is more noticeable in people with dark skin.

Vitiligo seems to be somewhat more common in people with certain autoimmune diseases, including hyperthyroidism (an overactive thyroid gland), adrenocortical insufficiency (the adrenal gland does not produce enough of the hormone called corticosteroid), alopecia areata (patches of baldness), and pernicious anemia (a low level of red blood cells caused by the failure of the body to absorb vitamin B12).

Scientists do not know the reason for the association between vitiligo and these autoimmune diseases. However, most people with vitiligo have no other autoimmune disease.

Vitiligo may also be hereditary; that is, it can run in families. Children whose parents have disorder are more likely to develop vitiligo. In fact, 30 percent of people with vitiligo have a family member with the disease. However, only 5 to 7 percent of children will get vitiligo even if a parent has it, and most people with vitiligo do not have a family history of the disorder.

Overcoming

I learned that the key to surviving is to accept who you are, your condition, and to love yourself. Living in shame is lonely and miserable way to live.

Shame is not my game anymore. But for many years I was not able to say that. I am proud of who I am. I'm proud to be able to understand my condition enough to help myself in so many different ways; I understand my symmetry now. I know when I'm pushing it too far and when I need to rest. You eventually learn to accept that you are different and that's the way people perceive you because that's the way it really is, and that's not about to change. You learn to get over it because life goes on.

Everything I just mentioned about being proud to understand my condition contains a key word: understand. There is not peace without understanding. It is impossible to obtain the calming effects of serenity unless there is awareness. To be aware is to be alert, to perceive, to grasp, and to appreciate.

Some of you out there may be experiencing your first spots or signs of vitiligo, and maybe this is devastating for you just like it was for me at first. My hope is that by reading this book and realizing that someone else has experienced, perhaps, worse trauma than you, you will be able to get through the dark times of changing faces. This is designed to give you comfort to know we have every right to enjoy our life to the fullest. We just learn to enjoy it in different ways but it can be done.

Here Are Some Suggestions That Worked For Me

1. Apply a sunscreen lotion to the exposed white spots before exposing to sunlight

2. Some persons with vitiligo receive benefits from a deliberate effort to tan the skin. A product called Trisoralen is first taken by mouth. Two hours later, the skin is exposed briefly to natural sunlight or to ultraviolet light. The procedure is repeated on subsequent days as the physician may direct.

3. A skin dye is sold under the trade name of DY-O-

Derm or neo-dyoderm. It is available in light and dark shades. It can be painted on the light skin areas to make them appear normal. For large areas, cosmetics such as Cover mark or eraser are useful.

Recreational Comfort that Worked for Me

Spiritual grounding is absolutely essential to lay a foundation for overcoming personal hardships in one's life. I attended church faithfully; not to make a name for myself as many churchgoers do, but I attended church to strengthen my belief in God. God is the beginning and the ending of all things and there is absolutely no way to get through life successfully without him!

Another recreational therapy that works for me is traveling. Whether its short or long distance, travel allows you to see many things. I can remember flying t Las Vegas for the first time. It was magnificent I had such a good time, and the trip was so therapeutic that I began using a travel agency to arrange a stay in Las Vegas once a year. You also get to see other people who are worse off that you. Then its easier to be thankful for your place in life.

I also enjoy parties, sports, and movies. Whenever I

was down, I threw a party! If being alone was to much to bear, guess what— a party was brewing.

Sports are recreations that I enjoy a lot. Driving to New Orleans or Jackson to see a game was nothing for me to do. Or I can cook a pot of my famous chili, settle back with refreshments, and watch football all day during the winter.

Watching a good movie always takes me way from difficult realities. It helps find things that can take you ways from worry and stress. Movies do that for me.

I adjusted to my condition during my skin change, but sometimes it was a little aggravation because I wanted to do more that I was able to do.

Misconceptions Are Often The Most Painful Part oF Vitiligo.

(Photos by Deste Lee)

Darrel Dabbs and Nora Denman both have vitiligo, a noncontagious condition that attacks the pigment of their skin.

By Michaela Gibson Morris
Daily Journal

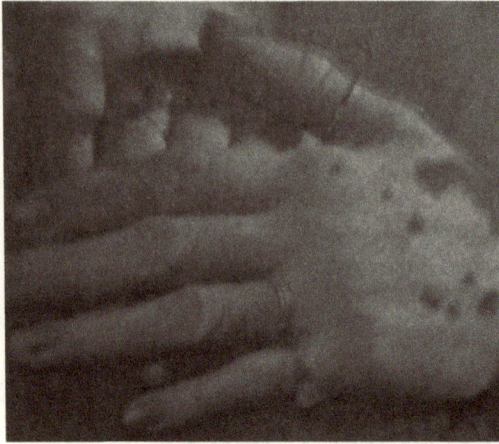

Nora Denman's Hands

Darrel Dabbs of Shannon and Nora Denman of Verona are used to the stares, curious inquires and occasional rude comments.

Unfortunately, they don't find many people who understand their pale skin is the result of vitiligo.

The relatively rare condition isn't contagious and it doesn't harm their health, but that hasn't stopped some people from being afraid to shake Darrel Dabbs' hands.

"Some people were afraid they were going to catch it," said Dabbs, 48, whose vitiligo has progressed so far that he has only a few spots of his original dark brown coloring.

Denman said she answers children and kind

questions gently and lest the other comments roll off her back

"I'm the same as they are," Denman 41, said. "My color is just not the same."

Autoimmune condition

Vitiligo is found in people of all different ethnic backgrounds, but it is most noticeable in people with darker skin tones.

"It's an autoimmune disease," said Tupelo dermatologist Dr. Jeff Houin. "The body is attacking the pigment cells.

The exact reason is not understood, but vitiligo isn't contagious and it doesn't affect the overall health of the person with the disease.

"It's not life-threatening like cancer," Dabbs said.

However, it can be a very difficult psychology because of its impact on self-image and identity.

"The part of it is very personal," Houin said.

Treatments take aim at controlling the immune system with topical corticosteroid creams and oral medications, Houin said. Specialized light therapy, which incorporates medication and thrice weekly light therapy sessions, have worked well for some. The frustration factor can be high.

"It can take 30 or 100 treatments before there's a response," with the light therapy, which cannot be used in small children, Houin said. "There's no great treatment."

The condition is most likely to surface in teens and young adults, but it can manifest itself at any age.

"For kids, it's touch because other kids are cruel," Houin said.

"They don't know what it is.

One of Houin's young patients made her vitiligo the center of her show-and tell. The teasing got better because her classmates understood what she was going through, he said.

Dabbs said he has made it his mission to spread the word about vitiligo in the hope of helping others.

"There's so many people out there hurting," Dabbs said.

Covering up

Dabbs wasn't quite a teenager when his vitiligo surfaced.

It showed up as a little patch around his eyes when he was in sixth grade, Dabbs said.

It spread to his lips, mouth, hands and then across his body.

For years, he wore makeup to avoid stares and heave a consistent skin tone. He had his lips tattooed so they wouldn't be pink.

"It made me look so much better," Dabbs said.

He'd get up at 5:30 a.m. to put the makeup on before work. He avoided eating in public and sometimes hugging people to avoid smearing it.

Dabbs decided against a treatment that would have bleached the pigment out of his skin.

"I was just hoping there'd be a cure," he said.

In 1997, he got sick and was hospitalized for an unrelated condition. But the toll on his immune system stimulated his vitiligo and almost all of his skin lost pigment.

Now his skin is all one pale color, except for a few spots on his chest, and he's occasionally mistaken for a white man.

Individualized Path

Denman's experience with the condition followed a different path and isn't as generalized as Dabbs.

"It was on the tips of my fingers for the longest," starting when she was a teen, Denman said.

In 1993 after she had her third child, the skin around her eyes and mouth and parts of her leg lost their pigment.

"It's stayed stable" since that time, she said.

While she occasionally wears makeup to church, she doesn't routinely cover up the spots on her face. She wears skirts and shorts when she wants to.

I had a speech impediment as a young child. It was more of a stutter that happened when I because overexcited and rushed t get words out. It was always a problem for me and caused me to shy away from people even more.

The combination of stuttering and skin discoloration caused me not to want to be around people at all unless I absolutely had to. However, being the worship leader at my church helped me to get rid of shyness. Nevertheless, I still could not see myself oun in public without makeup on my face.

My speech impediment didn't hinder me from doing a radio interview on 92 JAMZ radio station on a show called speak your piece, with Brandi Alexander. That was my first indication that I could do whatever I set my mind to do, and condition could not hold me back anymore.

In Closing

Regardless of how people look, if you want to know why they look a certain way, kindly ask them. Don't judge them or assume you know what's wrong with them; you most likely will put out the wrong report. Just ask.

Lots of people assumed that I had been burned because they didn't understand vitiligo, nor did they even now what it was.

All the effort I exerted and all the money I spent on makeup, trying to suntan, and other things this is definitely the character of a determined individual. Though my natural color never came back, I thank God that I'm alive and able to send a message of hope to the world through this book.

My health is not as good as I want it to be, but I do have a sound mind. Thank God! Perhaps if I could change things, I would , but I am able to accept things as they are. If you keep a sound mind and are willing to fight against the odds, you can overcome more than you'll ever imagine. I could have given up many times, but I didn't I'm still here. Again I say thanks be to God for giving me strength to fight when I thought I had no strength left to fight and when I thought I had very little to fight for.

To All My Vitiligo Sisters and Brothers

Be proud of yourself. Keep a sound mind, and don't ever give up. Keep fighting. I am hoping and praying that someday a cure will be found for vitiligo and not one will ever have to live in shame and denial because they look different from someone else. So what!

Life is truly uncertain, but karma is really real. You reap what you sow. But what do you do when you have a reap what someone else has sown? I grew up not knowing why I have vitiligo.

I am happy about all the things and ways that I have learned to take care of my condition. There are yet many unanswered questions regarding from where and whom my condition originated. I hope someday I will be able to answer these questions. The most important thing is to never give up and always keep your trust and confidence in yourself and in God. I don't believe I would be here today if I had not trusted God or if I had not trusted myself to do the right thing.

Trust yourself and trust God always. You really can do more than what your strength will allow you to do. When you go beyond your own strength, there is more on the other side of your strength. Don't worry about where it comes from; just embrace it, love it, and be happy. Take good care of yourself. Accept your condition, and don't be intimidated by others who stare at you or whisper when you pass by them. Being different will cause people to do those things; get over it as best you can.

People can be cruel. You must hold on to the memory and experience to meeting good people.

You cannot control anyone but yourself. Therefore, make sure you are being the best you that you can be. Rewards of good will be there when you need them. For now, while things are going well in your life, do unto others as you would have them do unto you.

www.ingramcontent.com/pod-product-compliance
Lightning Source LLC
Chambersburg PA
CBHW021828090426
42811CB00032B/2075/J